Periwinkle's Purpose

The Tale of a Snail

by Jody Trainor

Illustrations by Trudy Callbeck

Immense gratitude to those who generously shared their invaluable insights and encouragement.

Published By Periwinkle Press

ISBN: 978-1-0688970-1-6

To my sons, Jacob and Jamison.

May you always find comfort near the sea.

On the skirts of the tide I have traveled and seen,
dark troubled waters and places magically serene.

From my humble beginnings, clinging to stone.
To my worldly travels, destination unknown.

I am a grain of sand, in all my glory.

Take comfort, as I share my story.

A time ago in the mystic blue sea,
I once lived as a periwinkle as small as can be.

My shell was brightly colored, a ray of sun made it twinkle.
Life was pretty wonderful as a periwinkle.

The intricate path I'd weave across the sand,

Was a testament to this life I was destined to command.

Every glide came challenges both far and near,

but I was determined to persevere.

I moved with the sea,
to the beach and beyond.

I was tossed around by children,
making memories so fond.

I tumbled about in the waters swirling swish.

Triggered by schools of playing fish.

I witnessed the marvel of planktons glowing light,
created by a great blue whale's pass in the night.

All the wonders I had the pleasure to observe,
if only each moment, we could magically preserve.

I had touched so many lives and they touched mine.
Beautiful memories are what makes a life shine.

In the end, I sheltered in the kelp to stay out of harm's way.

I was so tired and knew I could no longer stay.

It was my time to die and for my life to move on.

I as a periwinkle, was gone.

Soon after, the sun would rise and start a new day.

Perhaps, my life as a periwinkle hasn't really gone away.

You may have seen me on the move, to a hermit crabs delight,

my shell turned a crab into a fearless knight.

My shell could also be spotted twirling and dancing in the waves.

Crashing on the rocks, my spirit echoed in caves.

Though my life as a periwinkle is no longer here,
my spirit is forever and always near.

Still part of the sea and now a speck of sand,
riding the tide, moving, and shifting the land.

I am the beach, I'm under your feet.

Constantly changing, one's life is never complete.

Remember, I am not just a spec of sand.

My living time on this earth, although short, it was grand.

So next time when at the beach, feel the sand between your toes.

Take time, and reflect on my story of how life ebbs and flows.

I'm still on a journey, into our world so divine,

leaving footprints of life and a legacy that will shine.

The End

Find rainbows in your tears when there are clouds in your sky,
and our loved one's spirit will never say goodbye.

www.ingramcontent.com/pod-product-compliance
Lightning Source LLC
Chambersburg PA
CBHW042115040426
42448CB00003B/279